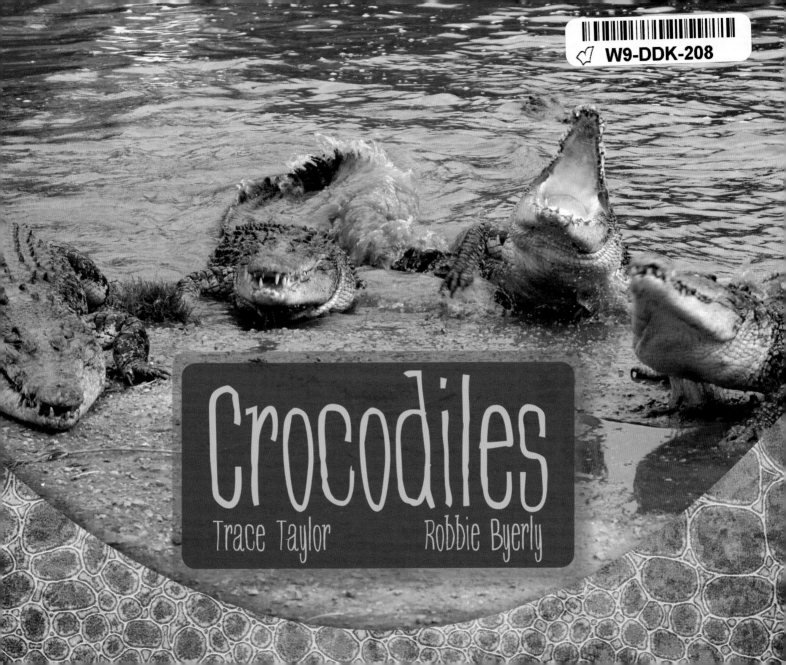

Crocodiles

Trace Taylor　　　Robbie Byerly

This is a crocodile.

3

Crocodiles can be as long as a truck.

Where Crocodiles Live

Look at this map. This map shows where crocodiles live. Crocodiles live where the map is red.

Crocodiles need the sun. They can't keep warm on their own. So they have to live where there is lots of sun. They have to live where it is hot.

Crocodiles need water. They can only
live where there is lots of water.

They spend most of their time under the water.

Crocodiles' eyes are on top of their heads.

This lets them see above the water when they are under the water.

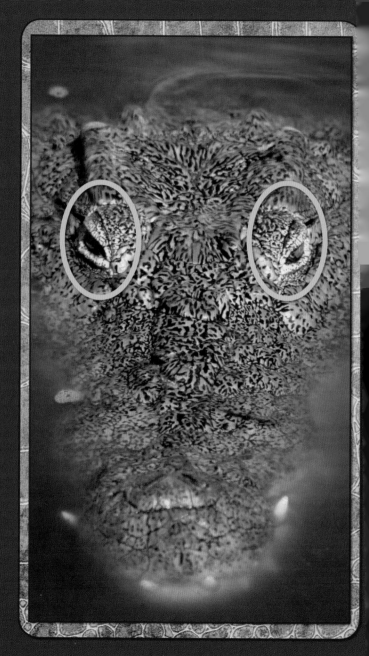

Crocodiles' noses are on top of their heads.

They can breathe air above the water when they are under the water.

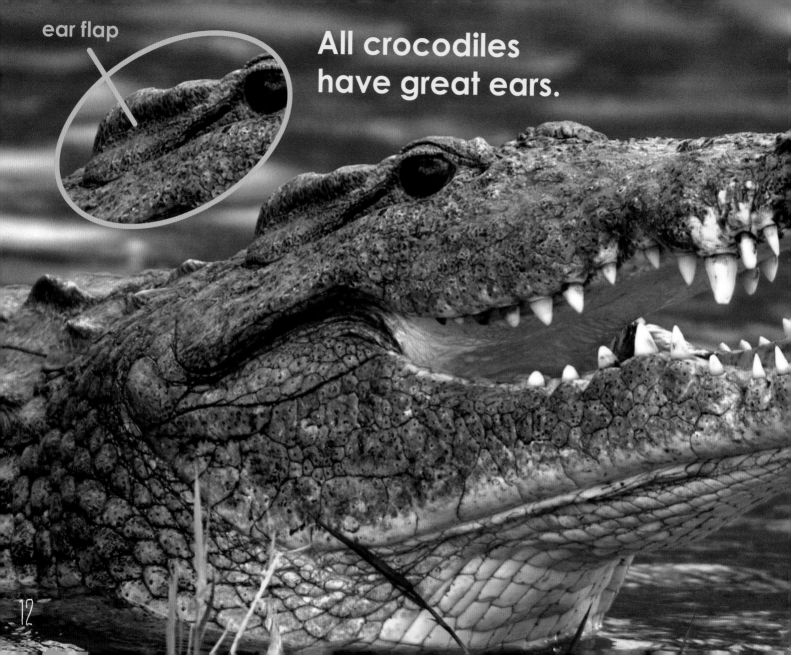

ear flap

All crocodiles
have great ears.

12

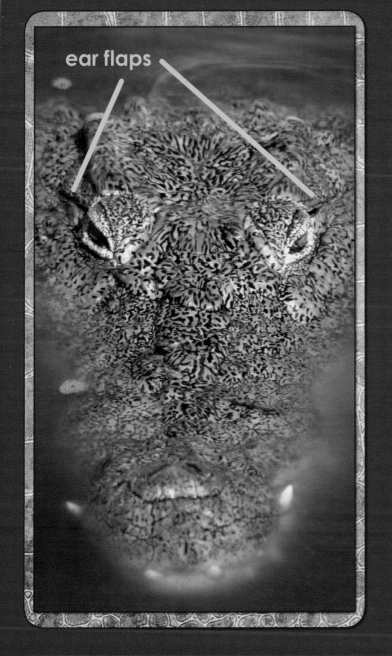

ear flaps

They can hear sounds above the water and under the water.

Crocodiles have tails.
Their tails have lots of spikes.

To swim, they swipe their tails from side to side. They are very fast. They can swim 25 miles an hour.

How Crocodiles Hunt

Crocodiles have to eat. They don't want to scare the animals away.

Crocodiles hide under the water. When an animal comes to drink, the crocodiles will sneak up on it.

17

Crocodiles use their tails to hit animals.

19

Crocodiles have long, sharp teeth. New teeth come in when old teeth fall out. A crocodile can have as many as 3,000 teeth in its life.

Crocodiles can shut their mouths fast.
Their teeth bite and hold.

Crocodiles eat lots of fish.

Crocodiles will eat all of these animals.

Big crocodiles can take down a zebra or a cow.

Big crocodiles will eat small crocodiles.

A Crocodile's Life Cycle

These are eggs.

These are bird eggs.

These are crocodile eggs.

Birds make nests.
Mother crocodiles make nests, too.
There can be up to 80 eggs in one nest.

When the babies come out of the eggs, they call to their mother.

She comes and gets the babies out of the nest.

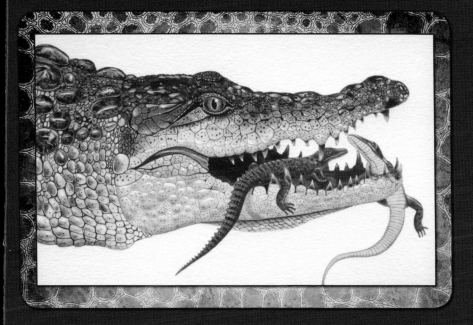

She takes the
babies with her.
They can ride
in her mouth.
They can ride
on her back.

These animals like to eat the baby crocodiles.
The baby crocodiles stay with their mother.
She keeps them safe.

The babies stay with their mother for two or three years. When they get big, these animals won't eat them.

In nine or ten years, the babies will be as big as their mother. So, look out!

The Crocodile's Life

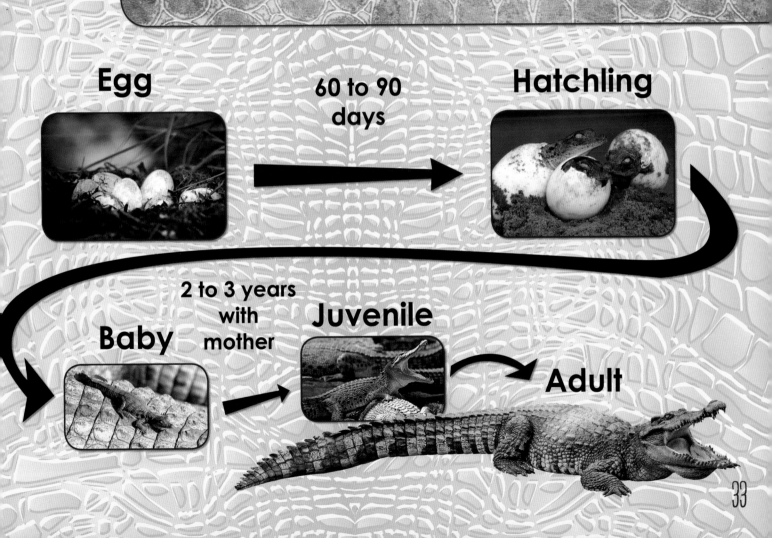

Egg

60 to 90 days

Hatchling

2 to 3 years with mother

Baby

Juvenile

Adult

Crocodile Anatomy

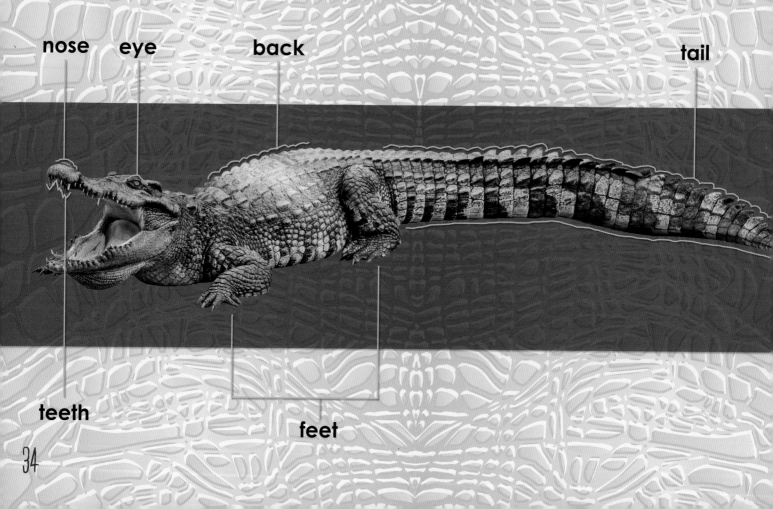

nose   eye   back   tail

teeth

feet

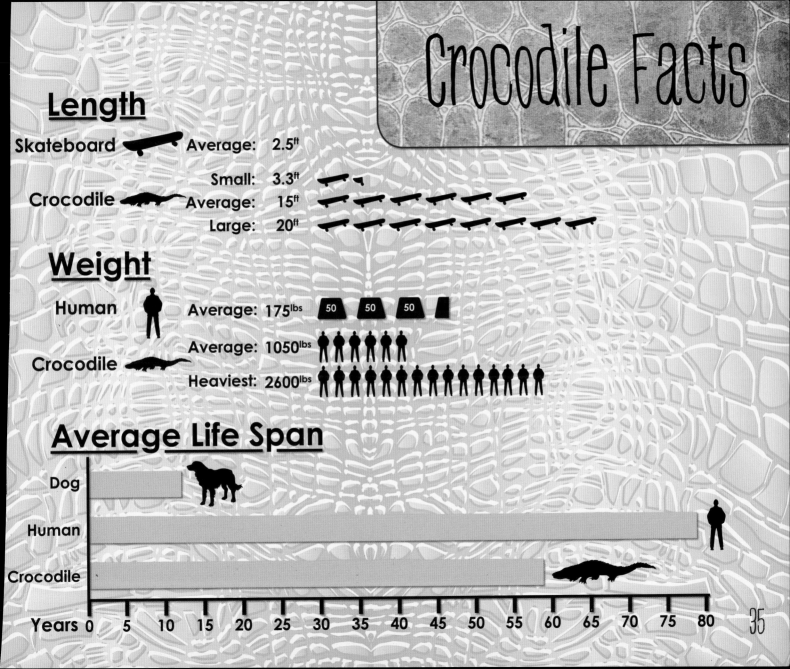

Crocodile Facts

Length

Skateboard — Average: 2.5ft

Crocodile —
- Small: 3.3ft
- Average: 15ft
- Large: 20ft

Weight

Human — Average: 175lbs

50 50 50

Crocodile —
- Average: 1050lbs
- Heaviest: 2600lbs

Average Life Span

Dog

Human

Crocodile

Years 0 5 10 15 20 25 30 35 40 45 50 55 60 65 70 75 80

35

Use words you know
to read new words!

it	play	make	all	old	eat
sit	lay	wake	ball	cold	sea
fit	hay	take	call	sold	seat
hit	stay	takes	small	hold	sneak

Tricky Words

away	long	only	people	use
great	old	own	their	very